JOURNEY
into the
Rainforest

Tim Knight

Photographs by Juan Pablo Moreiras
and Tim Knight

OXFORD
UNIVERSITY PRESS

For Estée - T.C.K.

OXFORD
UNIVERSITY PRESS

Great Clarendon Street, Oxford OX2 6DP

Oxford University Press is a department of the University of Oxford.
It furthers the University's objective of excellence in research, scholarship,
and education by publishing worldwide in

Oxford   New York

Auckland   Cape Town   Dar es Salaam   Hong Kong   Karachi
Kuala Lumpur   Madrid   Melbourne   Mexico City   Nairobi
New Delhi   Shanghai   Taipei   Toronto

With offices in

Argentina   Austria   Brazil   Chile   Czech Republic   France   Greece
Guatemala   Hungary   Italy   Japan   Poland   Portugal   Singapore
South Korea   Switzerland   Thailand   Turkey   Ukraine   Vietnam

Oxford is a registered trade mark of Oxford University Press
in the UK and in certain other countries

British Library Cataloguing in Publication Data available

Paperback ISBN 978-0-19-910731-5
9 10 8

Printed in Hong Kong

We gratefully acknowledge:

FAUNA & FLORA
International

Conserving wildlife since 1903

Great Eastern House, Tenison Road, Cambridge CB1 2DT, UK
www.fauna-flora.org

Fauna & Flora International acts to conserve threatened species and
ecosystems worldwide, choosing solutions that are sustainable, are
based on sound science and take account
of human needs.

Contents

Be Prepared

Rainforests are magical places. They are home to millions of amazing plants and animals: multi-coloured birds and iridescent butterflies; flying snakes and tree-climbing kangaroos; giant squirrels and miniature monkeys; bird-eating spiders and insect-eating plants; edible fungus and deadly poisonous frogs. There is something for everyone, especially if you like creepy crawlies!

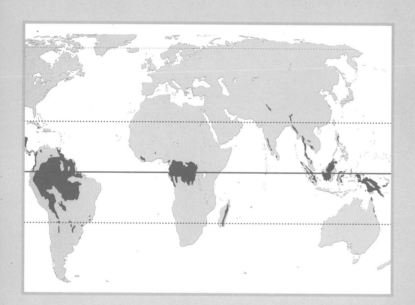

Rainforests are found mainly in the tropics. This area lies between two imaginary lines, known as the tropic of Cancer and the tropic of Capricorn, which run around the middle of the Earth. The Amazon rainforest in South America is probably the most famous, but there are other tropical forests in Africa, Asia, Central America and Australia.

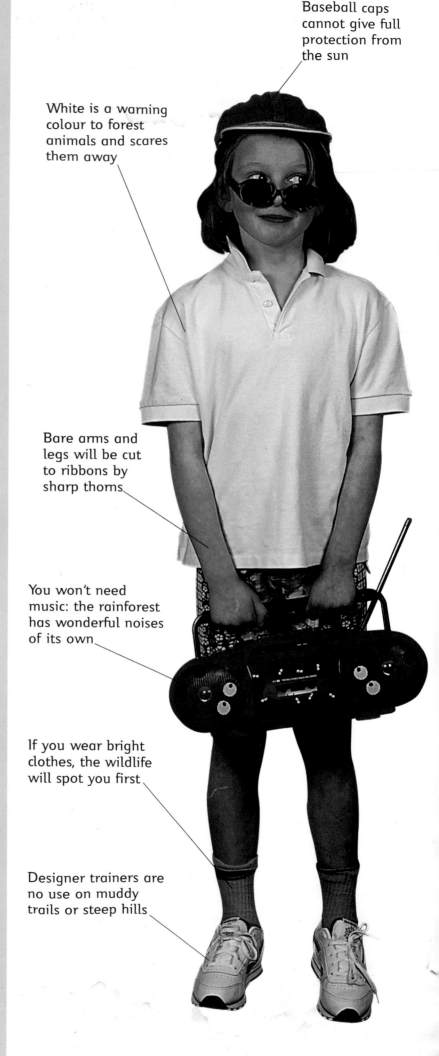

Baseball caps cannot give full protection from the sun

White is a warning colour to forest animals and scares them away

Bare arms and legs will be cut to ribbons by sharp thorns

You won't need music: the rainforest has wonderful noises of its own

If you wear bright clothes, the wildlife will spot you first

Designer trainers are no use on muddy trails or steep hills

4

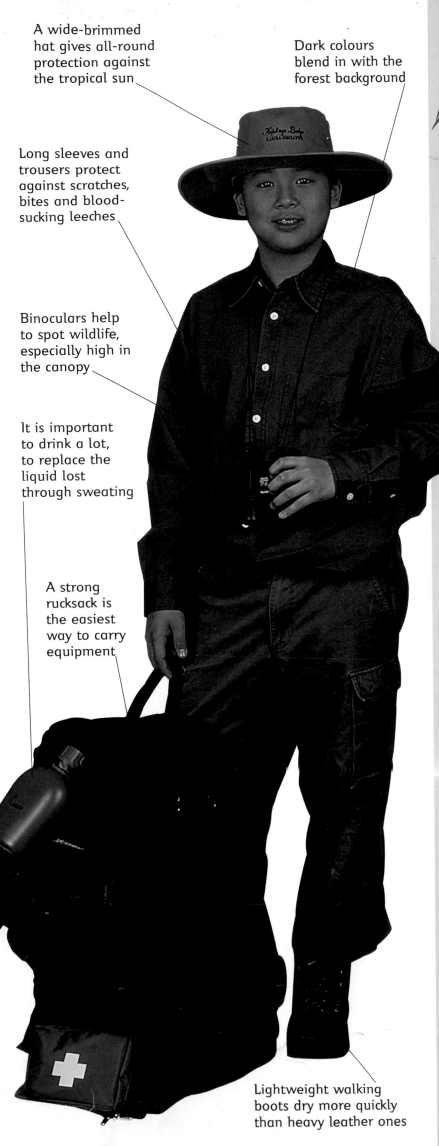

A wide-brimmed hat gives all-round protection against the tropical sun

Dark colours blend in with the forest background

Long sleeves and trousers protect against scratches, bites and blood-sucking leeches

Binoculars help to spot wildlife, especially high in the canopy

It is important to drink a lot, to replace the liquid lost through sweating

A strong rucksack is the easiest way to carry equipment

Lightweight walking boots dry more quickly than heavy leather ones

EVERY YEAR, an area of Amazon rainforest the size of Britain is destroyed.

The world's rainforests are all different, with their own special plants and animals, but they also have something in common: every one of them is full of wonderful surprises and hidden secrets, just waiting to be discovered. Unfortunately, all these forests are disappearing. Many countries that were once covered in forest have had the trees cut down either for timber or to make room for farms.

Visiting a tropical rainforest is an exciting experience, but it is also tiring, uncomfortable and even dangerous. Walking is hot and sticky work, the ground is often steep and muddy, and great care is needed to avoid stings, bites and scratches. To make the most of your trip you need to be fit, adventurous and well prepared. Top of the list is a visit to the doctor. No-one likes injections, but vaccinations give vital protection against many of the dangerous diseases that lurk in the forest.

It is also important to take the right clothes and equipment. This does not include personal stereos, computer games and the latest fashion! Are you ready to say goodbye to fizzy drinks, television, fast food and a warm bed? Have you remembered your passport? Stand by for the adventure of a lifetime!

5

Map of the Journey

Reaching the rainforest is an adventure in itself. It takes many hours – for some people days – to fly to the parts of the world where tropical forests are found. Even if there is a direct flight, the aircraft will often have to stop somewhere to refuel. Let's hope that there is no need to change planes as well. At least there will be plenty of time to dream about the forest and imagine what it is like.

By the time the plane finally arrives at its destination, you will already be a long way from home. This is where the real journey begins. From now on, every ride will be short and sweet: a bird's-eye view of the forest from a light aircraft; a speedboat trip as far as the last town; a bumpy ride in the back of a truck; travelling up the river by fishing boat; paddling upstream in a canoe. Every stage of the journey will take you closer to the heart of the forest, where the expedition on foot begins.

Bay

Landing Strip

Jetty

Banana Plantations

Mangrove Swamp

Market

Rice Fields

Village

River

Logged Forest

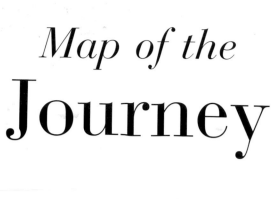

◀ The sun sets on a coastal fishing village.

▼ A bird's-eye view of the rainforest.

River

Logged Forest

Campsite

Night Walk

Waterfall

Walking Trail

Summit

Cloud Forest

Campsite

Into the Unknown

Imagine the small plane turning inland and flying above the tree-tops hundreds of metres below. As it comes in to land, there is dazzling blue sea on one side and a carpet of green rainforest on the other. The runway is just a thin strip of reddish earth among the trees. No wonder it is a bumpy landing. As the pilot opens the door, hot air rushes into the cabin. It is like being blasted by a big hairdrier. You have flown in three different planes just to reach the coast at the edge of the rainforest. For the next stage of the journey you need to travel by water.

▶ Most crocodiles are shy creatures. Sometimes all that you see is a beady eye.

A battered old speedboat is waiting by the jetty – its roof a piece of canvas held up by four poles. The boat is overloaded with people, wooden boxes and piles of bags. Climbing aboard, you notice an old lady holding a squawking chicken, wrapped in paper. The speedboat sets off towards the open sea. The bay is full of small fishing boats. As you pass them, a huge eagle flies down and grabs a big fish from the water. One of the fishermen smiles as he mends his net.

The boat follows the coast for a few minutes, then turns inland into a narrow, winding channel. Where it meets the sea, the river is salty and the water rises and falls with the tide. On either side are trees with their roots above the black mud. This is the mangrove swamp. It is low tide and the mangrove roots look like stilts, but at high tide they will be hidden under water.

Odd-looking fish are jumping around underneath the trees. They are called mudskippers, because they often leave the water and move about on land. Brightly coloured crabs wave to each other with an oversized claw. These are male fiddler crabs, showing off to impress the females.

Beyond the mangrove swamp, the channel becomes a wide river. Leaving the coast far behind, the boat races past banana plantations and tall palm trees. Eventually, it stops at a crowded jetty and everyone steps ashore.

▲ The trees and palms in a mangrove swamp are able to survive in salt water.

◀ At low tide, egrets walk around on the mud, searching for crabs and other food.

9

A Taste of Village Life

▲ River taxis are the best form of transport around this water village.

This is the last river port before the forest itself. Beyond the jetty is a noisy market, packed with people. Local farmers have come to town to sell their crops. You decide to follow them back to their village and continue your journey from there.

Walking in the baking heat is thirsty work. You stop to drink from your water bottle. A rusty old truck bounces past and stops to give the farmers a lift. As they jump in the back, they signal for you to join them. Taking a last gulp of water, you run to the truck and they pull you aboard. People are planting crops in the flooded fields that lie between the two rivers. The land is flat and bare, with hardly any trees. All the forest here has been chopped down and burned so that the people can grow rice and other food.

The road is just a dirt track. The ground is still very wet after a heavy rainstorm and the truck begins to slide around. Before long, one of the wheels sinks deep into the thick mud. The farmers jump down and throw rocks under the wheel. Then they all stand behind the truck and push together. As the wheels spin, everyone is sprayed with flying mud. The truck moves forward and the farmers jump back on.

You finally reach the village, but it seems deserted. All the grown ups are working in the fields, except for the oldest villagers and one or two mothers with babies. The houses are wooden huts, built on stilts to keep out animals and floods. Pieces of corrugated tin have been nailed on top to make a roof. Some small children are chasing a scrawny chicken. Two hungry dogs and a pig search for scraps of food under the huts.

◀ Who wants a banana split? A farmer carries his crop to market.

▶ The real, unspoilt forest begins far beyond where most humans live.

A flock of sleeping fruit bats is hanging in the trees. In the evening they will fly to the forest for a night feast.

It is time to resume your journey. One of the farmers takes you down to the river. He shouts to a fisherman, who steers towards the bank. Moving his nets to make room in the small boat, he invites you to climb in. The boat heads up-river towards the rainforest.

▶ During the day, fruit bats roost upside down in caves or trees.

Rain, Rain, Rain

The water is clear and fast flowing and the boat struggles against the strong current. The fisherman zigzags upstream, sticking to the deeper channels in order to avoid rocks and logs on the river-bed that could damage the boat's propeller. In some places the river is so shallow that you both have to jump into the water and push the boat. The river-bottom is very slippery and you fall over many times.

◀ A blue-banded kingfisher watches for lunch from its river-bank perch.

Where the river-bed slopes steeply and the surface of the water is broken by rocks, the current flowing in between them is even stronger. These parts of the river are called rapids. When the boat climbs a rapid, it seems to take forever to reach the top, just like trying to run up an escalator that is moving down.

Every few minutes the fisherman pulls in to the river-bank and stops to cast his net. He concentrates on the deeper pools below the overhanging vegetation. Fish gather here to feed on fruit or caterpillars that fall into the water.

◀ During heavy rain, soil is washed into the river, turning it muddy brown.

◀ Rain runs off the 'drip-tip' of a leaf, helping it to dry quickly before moss can form and block out the light.

It is growing darker. A storm is brewing. Thunder rumbles in the distance. Beyond the tree-tops up ahead, heavy rain is already falling. Soon the sky is almost black. When the rain finally comes, it is so heavy that you are drenched within seconds. The fisherman hauls in his net and pulls out the wriggling fish. By the time the boat sets off again, the rain is like a giant curtain and the opposite bank is invisible. Bigger and bigger branches float past, then small logs. The river is rising quickly and turning brown. As the water-level rises, loose material on the banks is being swept down the river. Objects stuck on the river-bed are being ripped loose by the powerful current.

As the boat reaches a bend in the river, it is met by a huge body of rushing water. The rain has caused a flash flood, racing down the swollen river like a tidal wave. Hold tight! For a moment, as the boat is lifted into the air, it feels as though it is bound to capsize. A massive log hurtles towards the boat like an out-of-control juggernaut. Just in time, the fisherman swerves out of its path. That was close! It is too dangerous to stay in the water, so the boat heads for the bank.

◀ In a violent rainstorm, up to ten centimetres of rain may fall in a single hour.

The Giant Umbrella

Safe at last! Someone else has found shelter here too. A small canoe is tied to a riverside tree. The flooded river has turned a caramel colour, as though someone has dumped hundreds of litres of melted chocolate into the water.

The sound of the rain is deafening as you enter the forest, but the tree-tops act like a giant umbrella. A thick layer of plants and leaves, called the canopy, covers the forest like a gigantic ceiling. The canopy plants absorb a lot of the heavy rain. Some water drips down, but it takes ten minutes to reach the forest floor.

If you are expecting to see a lot of wildlife, your first walk in the rainforest may be disappointing. Rainforest animals are shy and hard to find. Spotting them takes patience, luck and sharp eyes.

◀ The flower of a parasitic plant sprouts from a tree root on the dark forest floor.

▲ A bird's nest fern, growing on a platform of branches and winding stems in the canopy.

◀ Some butterflies have wings that seem to change colour in bright sunlight.

An iridescent butterfly flies past, then suddenly vanishes. As soon as it lands, it becomes invisible. With its wings closed, the butterfly is a dull brown colour, blending into the background.

The air feels hot and sticky, like a steamy bathroom. It is also quite dark. The tree-tops block out most of the light, even when the sun is shining. Plants cannot survive without sunlight, so there is not much undergrowth on the forest floor. There are thousands of small seedlings, most of them no more than a few centimetres tall. Bigger plants grow here and there. Palms with spiky stems and long, thin, many-fingered leaves can survive in shady places.

HIGH IN THE CANOPY the leaves of different trees never actually touch each other, even though they grow very close together. Scientists call this "canopy shyness".

It is growing even darker. As the fisherman leads the way through the trees, there is a smell of smoke. A little further into the forest, someone is sitting by a small fire. This must be the owner of the canoe. He signals you both to join him and points to himself: "Jali". This will be a good place to camp for the night.

▶ The deafening call of the "six o'clock" cicada is a sure sign that night is approaching.

The Night
has a Thousand Eyes

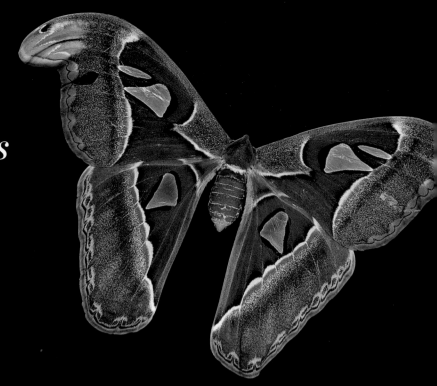

Darkness falls very quickly in a tropical rainforest. Nocturnal creatures, animals that come out at night, begin to wake up and call to each other. Birdsong gives way to the whistling of crickets and the frog chorus. After the heavy rain, the forest echoes with the gentle bleeping of tree frogs.

▲ The Giant Atlas, the world's biggest moth, lives in the rainforests of South-East Asia.

IT IS NEVER TOTALLY dark in the forest. The floor glows in certain places with the light from luminous fungi. Sometimes these fluorescent mushrooms seem to be suspended in mid-air, because they grow on tree-trunks that are almost invisible at night.

Nocturnal animals have different ways of finding food in the dark. Porcupines use smell to find fallen fruit on the forest floor. Forest cats have much better eyesight than humans and can hunt by moonlight. Some snakes can even find a mouse in the dark by sensing the heat from its body.

▼ A gecko emerges from its daytime hiding place to hunt for a meal.

Torchlight attracts hundreds of insects, including moths as big as dinner plates. The eyes of hidden spiders shine like pinpricks of light in the torch beam. In the distance, tiny flashing lights are moving through the trees. Fireflies! They are signalling to each other using a light at the end of their body, which flashes on and off like a neon sign.

A hungry gecko, a nocturnal lizard, scurries up a tree. Its beady eyes have spotted a cricket. A sticky tongue shoots out towards the juicy snack. Bull's-eye! There is a rustling sound overhead. A pair of red eyes stares down, blinking in the torchlight before disappearing among the leaves.

It has been a long day. You need to rest to prepare for the journey ahead. As you fall asleep, you wonder how many pairs of eyes are watching from the trees all around the camp.

▼ Luminous fungi are like mushrooms that glow in the dark.

Into the Heart of
The Forest

Next morning, even before sunrise, the birds and other forest creatures are making an amazing racket. Who needs an alarm clock? The forest is filled with whistling, singing, whooping and screeching.

It is time to check whether the river is safe again. Shake your muddy boots first. Something may have crawled into them during the night. Sure enough, a small scorpion falls out and scuttles away, its stinging tail held over its back.

▶ Scorpions catch prey with their claws and only use their poisonous sting in self-defence.

The river is still muddy, but the flood has gone down. Jali is waiting by the canoe. He points upstream, offering to take you into the heart of the forest. From now on, he will be your guide. The canoe passes huge trees that lean out over the water from both banks. As the river becomes narrower, the tree branches almost touch. In places, their leaves form an arch overhead, blotting out the sun. It feels as though the canoe is being pulled through the green tunnel by an invisible force, like a spaceship into a black hole.

◀ Roots spread out at the base of the trunk to support a tall tree.

▼ A deadly pit viper waits to ambush its victim.

On both sides, the walls of vegetation ring out with the voices of a thousand hidden creatures.

What is that low rumbling noise up ahead? The answer is around the next bend. A wall of water, higher than a house, blocks the way. The noise from the waterfall drowns all the other sounds.

Jali paddles to the bank, ties the canoe to a tree and unloads the bags. He starts climbing up the steep bank next to the waterfall, inviting you to follow. The ground is slippery because of the spray, making the climb even tougher.

Pausing for breath at the top, you look back down at the river, hoping that the canoe will still be there when you return. If it is swept away by the next flood, there is no way back.

▶ Birdwing butterflies gather on the wet mud to feed on minerals.

▲ The damp conditions near a waterfall are ideal for moisture-loving plants, frogs and other wildlife.

19

Brilliant Trees

As you walk into the forest, a tiny yellow and red kingfisher takes off from a nearby branch and flies ahead like a brightly coloured dart.

Watch your step! It is easy to trip over the tree roots that grow along the forest floor, stretching out like big veins. Rainforest trees do not have deep roots. All the moisture and goodness they need is near the soil's surface, among the wet carpet of rotting leaves known as the leaf litter. Without deep roots to support their massive trunks, the trees are top-heavy. To stop themselves from falling, especially in strong winds, they grow special roots, called buttresses. Buttress roots fan out from the sides of the trunk, a couple of metres from the base, giving the tree extra support like stabilisers on a bicycle.

▶ Not all kingfishers eat fish. This species lives deep in the forest, feeding on insects and spiders.

▶ The nibung palm tree protects itself with a shield of vicious spikes.

20

◄ Most rainforest trees are covered with climbing plants.

Near the Equator, where tropical rainforests are found, it is wetter, warmer and sunnier than anywhere else in the world, and the climate has hardly changed for tens of millions of years. This is a perfect place for trees and plants to grow, like an endless greenhouse stretching all the way around the middle of the Earth.

Some of the gigantic trees towering above you have lived for centuries. Their massive trunks are straight and smooth, stretching all the way into the tree-tops. It feels as though you are standing next to giant stone pillars in a cathedral.

Suddenly, there is a loud cracking noise, like a gunshot, followed by a huge crash. Somewhere close by, a big tree has fallen. Everything goes quiet, as though the whole forest has stopped to listen. This is a great chance to see some of the plants that normally grow out of sight in the tree-tops. You set off in the direction of the crash.

TROPICAL RAINFORESTS are filled with a dazzling variety of trees. Many of them look the same, but an expert can find over 100 different kinds in an area the size of a football pitch.

Reach for
The Sky

Ashort distance ahead, sunlight is shining down into the forest and lighting up the tree-trunks. This must be where the tree has fallen. You step out of the darkness into a brightly lit area criss-crossed with fallen trees, broken branches and strange-looking plants. The biggest tree has a coating of wet moss. Huge ferns and other plants are still clinging to its top branches. There are orchids too, with pretty white flowers. Orchids need a lot of light, so they usually grow in the canopy, where their roots take in water from the damp air.

◀ More than three-quarters of the world's orchids grow in rainforests.

Trees often fall after a long storm. All the leaves and climbing plants in the top of an old tree are soaking wet, and the extra weight of the water in the crown of the tree becomes hard to support. If the load is too heavy, the whole tree crashes to the ground.

◀ Sunlight floods through a gap in the canopy where a tree has fallen.

The massive tree has flattened everything in its path, snapping the trunks of smaller trees as if they were matchsticks. There is a big patch of blue sky overhead. It looks as though someone has punched a gigantic hole through the roof of the forest. Bright sunshine is pouring into the big gap, lighting up the ground like a giant searchlight.

▶ A chance in a million. Tiny seedlings need a lot of luck to survive.

▼ A young plant soaks up the sun's rays. The race to the canopy has just begun.

When an old tree falls, it destroys some life and creates other new life. Plants and animals lose their tree-top home, or are crushed in the fall. Meanwhile thousands of seeds and young plants, warmed by the sun, spring into life and begin a race for the sky. One of them will grow to fill the gap left by the fallen tree. The race is a marathon, lasting many years. Some plants will start like sprinters, growing quickly, but only for a short time. When these "pioneers" can grow no taller they will be overtaken, leaving the long-distance runners to battle for the finishing post. It could be thirty years before the winner reaches the top and spreads its branches, blocking out the sunshine once more.

Your head begins to throb. It is time to shelter from the blazing heat. Jali has already found an umbrella. He holds an enormous leaf over his head as he leads the way back into the shade of the forest.

▲ Wild bananas grow quickly. They are one of the first plants to colonize a gap in the forest.

All Creatures
Great and Small

Stepping back into the dark forest, Jali stops in front of a rotting log. From a distance it seems to be covered in small flowers. In fact, the brightly coloured patches sprouting from the log are a type of fungus. Fungus is a simple plant that spreads quickly through the leaf litter on the humid forest floor. It feeds on dead leaves and old wood, causing them to decay and rot more quickly.

▶ Pill millipedes curl into a ball to protect themselves.

This log still looks solid, but when you press it, the surface is soft and spongy under your fingers. There is no gap in the canopy overhead, which means that this tree fell long ago. It takes years for a big log to decay, but eventually it will disappear without a trace, eaten away by fungus, millipedes, beetles and other creatures.

A snail has been feeding on the fungus. It begins to crawl away slowly, then suddenly stops and pulls in its horns.

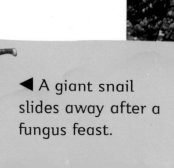

◀ A giant snail slides away after a fungus feast.

▲ Bracket fungus sprouts from a decaying branch on the forest floor. Fungi that feed on dead wood are called saprophytes.

Something is blocking the snail's path. A stream of tiny ant-like creatures is crossing the log. Termites! Thousands of them, marching along like miniature soldiers in an unbroken line.

▶ Termite mounds have strong, hard walls made out of droppings, saliva and soil.

A termite is smaller than a matchhead, but it is one of the most important creatures in the rainforest. Termites have found a way to turn rotting leaves and dead wood into food. They recycle all the "rubbish" in the forest by taking it home and eating it! Day and night, they race around like six-legged vacuum cleaners, hoovering up bits of the forest. While the termites are doing this, the bigger animals eat them! In the rainforest, everything ends up being eaten by something else.

The termites are breaking up the log and carrying it away, piece by piece. The termite trail winds along the ground for over a hundred metres, then climbs a small tree before disappearing into a tube of dried mud. This is the termites' home. Somewhere inside is the giant queen, hundreds of times bigger than the workers who look after her. Every day she lays thousands of eggs.

▲ A stick insect flattens itself against a branch until the danger has passed.

Hide and Seek

Just beside the trail of termites, one of the dead leaves on the floor starts to move. How can a leaf blow if there is no wind? The leaf moves again, then suddenly flies away. It's a moth in disguise! How many more of these leaves are alive? You stare at a patch of ground, waiting for something else to move. There! A walking twig? No. A stick insect. It folds all six legs against its body and lies completely still, invisible again.

▲ Thanks to the false holes on its wing cases, this cricket looks like a half-eaten leaf.

Rainforests are full of hidden creatures that survive by pretending to be something else. They wear a disguise in order to fool predators, the animals that hunt and kill them. The clever disguises that they use are known as camouflage.

It takes sharp eyesight to spot a camouflaged animal in the forest. Jali finds a frog hidden among a pile of dead leaves. The trees, plants and forest floor are alive with hundreds of creatures looking like hopping leaves, flying sticks, and six-legged pieces of wood.

◄ The Bornean Horned Frog can sit perfectly still for hours on end, disguised as a pile of leaves.

Camouflage is a good way to avoid being eaten, but it can also help the predators to catch food: a leopard's spots help it to blend in with the background as it hunts; the stem of a plant may really be a thin green snake, waiting to ambush a careless bird. Smaller predators are just as clever. The flower mantis, a fierce insect, catches food by pretending to be a flower. Parts of its body look like flower petals. When an insect is tricked into landing, the mantis grabs it, eats the juicy bits, then waits for the next visitor. In the rainforest, hide and seek is not a game, it is a matter of life and death.

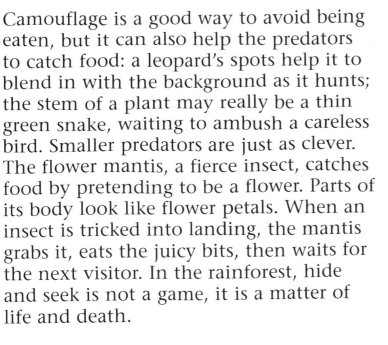

▲ Now you see me, soon you won't! Could you spot this stick insect on a mossy tree trunk?

Some animals are so hard to see that only an expert can find them. Often, the only sign of their presence is a noise in the trees, a feather on the ground or a footprint in the mud. To read the signs, you need to be a forest detective.

▼ This well-camouflaged moth looks like the dead leaves that it rests on.

Beauty and
The Beasts

The forest is full of clues. There are marks in the mud beside a nearby puddle. An animal has been drinking here. A short trail of hoofprints leads away from the water but they fade where the ground is harder. Jali finds a piece of fur left behind on a sharp branch. This way! Walking on tiptoe, he avoids the dry twigs that would snap loudly if he trod on them. He stops. Just a few metres away, lying completely still, is a baby deer.

▲ The eyes of a chameleon can move in different directions at the same time.

▶ When frightened, a baby barking deer bleats loudly. The adult deer barks like a dog.

A blue feather floats to the forest floor from the canopy. Jali looks up and whistles. He is imitating the call of a bird. Within seconds a bright blue bird appears, whistling loudly. Here is the owner of the feather. Mistaking Jali for another bird, it has flown down to defend its territory, the part of the forest where it lives.

◀ This flycatcher from South-East Asia can be tempted into the open by people imitating its call.

◀ The skin of the poison dart frog oozes deadly poison. Forest hunters use it on the tips of their blowpipe darts.

Jali picks up something that looks like a big toothpick. It is a porcupine quill, stiff and needle-sharp. Porcupines are like giant rats, protected by a coat of pointed spines.

A colourful frog is sitting by a pool of rainwater. It may look pretty, but picking it up is not a good idea. Brightly coloured animals are often poisonous. This warns predators to keep away. Others use bright colours to trick their enemies. They pretend to be dangerous by copying the appearance of a poisonous animal. This is called mimicry. To avoid being eaten, some harmless butterflies mimic the warning colours of a bad-tasting species.

▲ Many heliconid butterflies taste bad. Birds quickly learn to leave them alone.

▼ Despite its bright warning colours, this striped bronzeback snake is harmless.

There is a rustling sound in the leaf litter. Is it a lizard? Take a closer look. Curled up on the forest floor, almost invisible among the dead leaves, is a small viper. This deadly snake does not want to be seen. When trying to ambush your next meal, camouflage is more important than warning away an enemy.

Survival *in the* Forest

The smallest creatures are often the most dangerous. Every year, thousands of people in tropical countries die from malaria. This disease is spread by mosquitoes while they are drinking your blood.

▶ Fruit comes in all shapes and sizes, but it is not always edible.

People who live in the rainforest cannot afford modern medicine to cure sickness. Instead they rely on forest plants. In some tropical forests the people treat malaria by drinking quinine, made from the bark of the cinchona tree.

Many of the trees and plants in Jali's forest have important uses. He may boil leaves and drink the liquid to cure a fever. Certain roots can be cooked like a vegetable. Some palms have strong fibres that are used for weaving.

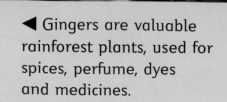

◀ Gingers are valuable rainforest plants, used for spices, perfume, dyes and medicines.

▶ There are no taps in the forest, but you can find water in a liana stem.

Jali passes you a piece of fruit. It smells bad, but you decide to taste it. Delicious! You find some juicy-looking berries, but Jali shakes his head. They are poisonous. Pressing his ear up against a fallen tree, he taps the rotten trunk, then listens. He grins and pokes a stick into a hole in the rotting wood, before pulling out two fat, white grubs. He eats one and offers you the other. Close your eyes and swallow quickly!

You take out your water bottle, but Jali has a better idea. He reaches up to the thick wooden stem of a liana, hanging down from the tree-tops. Lianas are huge climbing plants. They grow up into the canopy by winding around other plants and using them for support. Jali cuts the liana. A stream of water gushes out of the stem.

People like Jali spend their whole life in the forest. They depend on it for food, medicine and shelter. Without the forest, they would have no home.

▲ A quarter of all the world's medicines come from rainforest plants.

▲ This spike of berries belongs to a forest herb.

31

Trunk Roads

Water is still dripping from the end of the liana. The long stem twists and turns upwards, disappearing among the tangle of leaves high above. Through a gap in the canopy, Jali spots a big honeycomb. It is hanging from beneath a high branch near the crown of a giant tree. The tree-trunk is smooth and straight, with no low branches. Is he really going to climb that? First he cuts down a sapling, to use later as a long pole. Ignoring the giant tree, he walks to the next tree-trunk instead.

◄ A dragon lizard waits patiently for a passing meal of termites or ants.

It is covered with lianas that have hitched a ride to the canopy. Jali uses their winding stems as a ladder. Within minutes, he reaches the crown of the tree and waves for you to follow. What are you waiting for? This is no time to be scared of heights. Now's your chance to find out what the canopy really looks like.

► Cauliflorous trees, which produce flowers directly from their trunks, are only found in rainforests.

The part of the forest between the floor and the canopy is called the understorey. A few animals spend all their time here, but most are just passing through. Squirrels, ants and termites use the tree-trunks as roads between the ground and the tree-tops. The climbing plants are on the move too, trying to reach the sunlight high above. Many of the smaller climbing plants have curved spines on their stems and leaves. These help them to hook on to branches as they spiral upwards.

◀ A flying lizard in the hand, showing how it turns its rib-cage into "wings".

A few metres above the ground, the trunk passes through the crowns of one or two smaller trees. Above them, there is a good view of other big trunks. In a nearby tree, a lizard is being chased by a snake. Suddenly, it launches itself into the air and glides down on to another trunk. Flying lizards turn themselves into miniature hang-gliders by stretching out their ribs like a pair of stiff wings. Other rainforest animals have learnt to fly: gliding frogs use their webbed feet as parachutes; some squirrels have loose flaps of skin on their sides; flying snakes flatten their bodies into a winding ribbon.

Higher still, closer to the sunlight, the tree begins to spread out its thick crown of leaves. Just below the canopy, long roots dangle down in mid-air. They belong to the tree ferns and other plants that have made their home in the branches. Don't look down!

◀ Most old tree trunks are coated in moss and climbing plants.

The *Canopy* World

There is a crashing noise in the branches as you reach the top. A monkey leaps into the next tree... then another, and another. The branches are full of fruit, and the monkeys are having a feast. A nearby tree is covered in small flowers; swarms of insects are feeding on the nectar; tiny green birds hop among the leaves. Meanwhile, multicoloured parrots with red, green and blue feathers fly noisily through the tree-tops. The air is filled with the sound of buzzing, howling, squawking and twittering.

▶ South American spider monkeys use their tails as an extra arm to hang from trees.

Some birds are eating fruit; others search for caterpillars, or uncover spiders and beetles by turning over the dead leaves that have piled up in the forks of branches. Because of the warm and damp conditions, the leaves rot quickly and produce nutrients – a kind of natural fertiliser. This unlimited supply of food and water means that many plants can survive high up in the trees, clinging on to branches or tree-trunks instead of sending their roots into the soil on the forest floor. Plants that grow in this way are called epiphytes. Tree frogs hide among epiphytes during the day and even lay their eggs in the tiny pools of water that are trapped in these plants after it rains.

▲ The early morning mist evaporates as the forest is warmed by the sun's rays.

◄ Water collects in a bromeliad high above the ground, forming a miniature pond for tadpoles.

Reaching the canopy is like discovering a store of hidden treasure. It is filled to bursting point with wildlife, sheltered from the baking sun by the thick layer of leaves. No wonder it is difficult to see animals down on the forest floor – most of them live in this giant roof garden, thirty metres above the ground! More than three-quarters of all rainforest creatures spend their whole life high in the canopy. Up here, the plants and animals have everything they need: food, water, sunlight, shade and shelter. Over thousands of years, they have become experts at living in the tree-tops, so they never need to leave their home in the sky.

▶ Although toucans can fly, they prefer to hop from branch to branch in search of food.

Above the Canopy

Higher still, above the roof of the forest, the air is fresher and the light is dazzling. After the dark and damp of the forest floor, the view from the top takes your breath away. The forest canopy looks like an enormous green carpet stretching as far as the eye can see.

Here and there, single giant trees grow up through this carpet, like spindly toadstools on a big garden lawn. These trees are called emergents. Some grow more than fifty metres tall, higher than a block of flats. A huge honeycomb is hanging from a thick branch in the crown of one of these trees.

◄ A gigantic emergent tree towers above the rest of the forest canopy.

Apart from the distant mountains, this is the highest point for many kilometres. The forest stretches out of sight in all directions. Some of the tree-tops below have bare branches. Rainforests have strange seasons of their own. Trees drop their leaves and grow new ones, but not all at the same time. Every species is different.

A massive eagle perches close to its nest in the crown of another giant tree. These huge, powerful birds eat monkeys. Eagles are the kings of the canopy with nothing to fear from other animals, except man himself. Below them, the forest is like a big dining room where all the guests are busy eating each other.

Plants and animals are linked by what they eat and what eats them. Biologists call this a "food web". Even the fiercest predator ends up as food for something else. When an eagle dies, it may be eaten by scavengers, or its body may just rot in the soil and turn into plant food. Nothing goes to waste in the rainforest.

Giant bees build their nests high above the ground to protect their honey from thieves. They often choose the tallest trees in the forest, well beyond the reach of creatures with a sweet tooth. Only the very bravest or hungriest animals would risk such a dangerous climb. Jali has found a better way to reach the honey in the next tree. Using the pole that he made earlier, he leans across and tries to knock down part of the honeycomb. He takes care not to destroy the whole nest, so that the bees will stay here after he has finished.

◄ The South American harpy is the world's largest eagle.

37

Down to
Earth

▲ Birds that drink nectar are attracted by bright colours, especially orange and red.

Above the sheltered canopy, the wind is blowing quite strongly. Seed pods break loose from the branches in the emergent tree. They fall slowly, spinning like helicopter blades. The wind blows them a long way from the giant tree, giving them a chance to spread to different parts of the forest.

▶ Seeds with wings rely on the wind to blow them long distances.

Lower down inside the canopy, the air is still. Without wind to spread their seeds, trees rely on birds, insects, or bigger animals to do the job. To attract them, they produce sweet-tasting, strong-smelling fruit and flowers that are brightly coloured and filled with nectar.

When a bird or insect reaches into a flower to drink nectar, its head is covered in a sticky dust, called pollen. As it lands on another flower, this pollen rubs off. If both flowers are the same kind, the second plant will grow seeds. Bigger animals eat fruit, then move to another part of the forest. The seeds hitch a ride in the animal's stomach, before being left behind in its droppings. Different types of trees produce flowers, fruit, or seeds at different times of the year, so food is always available somewhere.

Beneath the clinging lianas, the tree seems to have more than one trunk. In fact, there are two trees. Most of the "trunks" are thick roots belonging to an old strangler fig that has wrapped itself around the trunk of another tree. The supporting tree is known as the host. This strangler fig did not grow up from the ground. It started life as a seed in the tree-tops after being dropped there by a bird. When a fig seed sprouts in the fork of a branch, it quickly sends long, thin roots down to the ground. Other roots grow down through the host tree, criss-crossing its trunk in a thick mesh. As the fig tree grows stronger, its crown of leaves spreads through the canopy, producing fruit for the next generation of birds and monkeys. One day, this crown will overshadow the host tree, blocking out its light. The host tree may die, but by then the strangler fig is strong enough to support itself.

Down on the ground, butterflies are feeding on the fallen fruit. After dark, fruit bats, deer, and wild pigs will join the feast. A fig tree in fruit is like a free banquet that takes place just once a year. The animals around it feed day and night until the food runs out.

▼ Rotting fruit produces alcohol. This Tufted Jungle Queen butterfly is already drowsy after sampling a fallen fig.

▲ The roots of an old strangler fig wrap themselves around the host tree like a strait-jacket.

The *Jigsaw* Puzzle

Rainforests have existed for millions of years. During that time, plants and animals have filled every available space and worked out the best way to live in their forest home. After existing side by side for so long, many animals and plants have come to depend on each other for survival. All living things in the rainforest are connected. The system that connects them is known as an ecosystem.

Leaning on a fallen log to rest after the climb down, you brush against a tall plant. Within seconds, your arm is covered with biting ants. The colony lives in the plant's hollow stem and feeds on a sweet, sticky substance produced by its leaves. In return, the ants protect the plant from many leaf-eating creatures. Ant and plant live in perfect harmony, helping each other to survive.

▼ Chopping down just one tree can destroy the habitat of many plants and animals.

The rainforest ecosystem fits together like a living jigsaw puzzle. If any piece of the puzzle is missing, the whole jigsaw is ruined. When one kind of plant or animal becomes extinct, everything else that depends on it will die too.

▶ Some flowers depend on a particular type of insect to spread their pollen

Just as each piece of a jigsaw will only fit into one part of the puzzle, every animal and plant has its own special place, known as a habitat. Plants that need bright sunlight cannot live on the dark forest floor.

▼ ▶ A single tree-top epiphyte provides a permanent home for small creatures such as tree frogs.

A hungry caterpillar will starve if it strays far from its foodplant. Tadpoles cannot survive without water. The ecosystem is made up of thousands of small habitats. For example, the crown of every tree is like a miniature city, with its own population of permanent residents. Visitors such as monkeys, birds and insects may come and go, moving from town to town in search of food, but some creatures spend their entire life in the same tree-top home. They can never move away, because they rely on the other plants and animals in the neighbourhood.

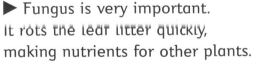

▶ Fungus is very important. It rots the leaf litter quickly, making nutrients for other plants.

◀ Pitcher plants rely on a diet of insects, without which they could not survive in poor soil.

The distant mountains, visible only from high above the canopy, provide shelter for some plants and animals that are found nowhere else in the forest. Reaching them is difficult, but Jali knows the safest way.

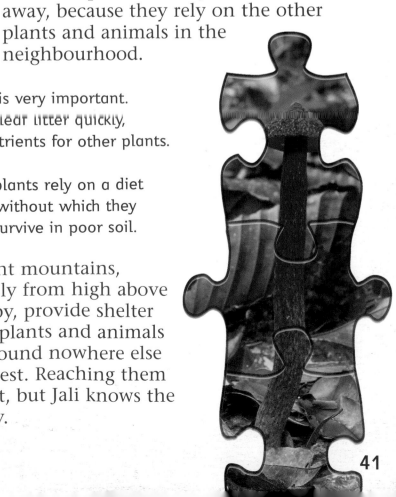

Head in the Clouds

Jali leads the way up into the hills. He seems to be following a path that is invisible to anyone else. It is hard to walk here because the ground is becoming steeper. As you climb higher, the temperature begins to turn colder. The air is very damp and misty. The canopy overhead is lower. Even the tallest trees are no higher than a house. Most of this forest is made up of smaller trees and shrubs.

► The spiderhunter's bill helps it to feed on nectar and insects that other birds cannot reach.

Most of the plants up here are different from those lower down in the valley. Something else has changed too. The forest is quieter. There is not much birdsong or insect noise. When birds appear, they look different too. This may be the only place in the whole forest where they can be seen. In some places, the way is blocked by twisted trunks covered with a thick mesh of sharp-spiked climbing plants.

◄ This lizard, a small skink, can live in the hills, but it is too cold for many reptiles.

▲ Most orchids are epiphytic, with flowers that hang down from the tree branches.

Water is dripping from the wet moss that hangs from the branches and clings to the tree-trunks. The moss is also growing on the ground, covering the rocks, roots and forest floor in a spongy, slippery carpet. Patches of thick mist drift through the forest. The atmosphere is eerie. Ghost-like shapes appear and disappear. Trees stretch out their mossy arms, ready to tap you on the shoulder as you pass by. Beautiful, pale orchids dangle from the branches, brushing your face.

There is a scuffling sound in the undergrowth. A long snout pokes out, followed by some whiskers and a furry face. The face belongs to a huge rat. Unafraid, it stops to sniff the air and take a good look at the two-legged intruders, before vanishing into a thick bush. The last thing to disappear is its long tail, thicker than a bootlace.

Jali points through the trees towards an orange glow in the distance. The sun is already setting. It is time to rest for the night. The climb to the summit will have to wait until the morning.

▲ Dense forest covers a hillside.

On Top of The World

The night is so cold that it is hard to sleep. You are awake before dawn. As soon as the sun begins to rise, you set off once more, climbing slowly. It is hard to breathe, because there is less oxygen up here. The mountain is still buried under heavy cloud.

Most of the trees are short and stubby, growing sideways rather than upwards. Their growth is restricted by the strong winds and the poor soil.

Winding through the low bushes there are long stems ending in leaves shaped like miniature vases. Normal plants obtain food from the soil. These pitcher plants are different. They catch insects instead! If an ant crawls into the pitcher, the slippery walls stop it climbing out again. The liquid inside the pitcher is a mixture of rainwater and chemicals. When the ant falls in, it is dissolved and turned into plant food.

◄ Deforestation destroys one acre of the world's rainforests every second.

The summit is covered in ferns and other low-growing vegetation. As you reach the top, the morning mist is beginning to clear. On all sides, patches of green start to appear, like glimpses of colour seen through spy-holes on a steamed-up window. Soon there is nothing but dazzling forest, stretching to the horizon in every direction.

In the distance, a plume of smoke rises from a massive area of bare earth, where the forest is being logged and burned. It looks like a giant cigarette burn on a precious carpet. The world's rainforests are being destroyed. One day, the rest of this forest may disappear too, along with all the wonderful creatures in it.

An eagle appears overhead. It swoops down into the valley, soaring high above the canopy where the monkeys are just waking up, and flies towards the coast. Soon it is just a distant speck in the sky, gliding over the airstrip where your incredible rainforest journey began.

▶ Pitcher plants trap and eat insects, or even small lizards.

Glossary

bromeliad A kind of epiphyte found in tropical America

buttress roots Flat roots that grow out sideways from the trunk, above the ground, to stop tall trees from falling over

camouflage A disguise that helps an animal to hide

canopy The layer of leaves and branches in the tree-tops that forms a roof over the forest

cauliflorous The scientific word to describe trees that grow flowers or fruit straight from their trunks, not from their branches

cicada A noisy insect that calls by rattling the sides of its body hundreds of times a second

deforestation The disappearance of trees when forests are chopped down or burned

dormant As if asleep

drip-tip Long point at the end of a leaf that helps rainwater to drain away quickly

ecosystem The way that living things are connected and depend on each other for survival

emergents Tall trees that grow higher than the rest of the forest and stick out above the canopy

epiphyte A plant that grows on another plant, using it only for support

evaporate Change from liquid to gas

extinct Describes a plant or animal that no longer exists

fluorescent Glowing brightly

food web The relationship between animals and plants that eat each other

fungi Simple plants with no flowers, leaves or roots, found in dark, damp places

gap colonizers Plants that are the first to grow in the open space after a tree falls

gecko A kind of lizard, usually nocturnal

habitat The place where an animal or plant lives

host A plant or animal used by a parasite to help it feed or grow

iridescent With dazzling colours that change in the sunlight

leech Harmless, blood-sucking worm

liana Climbing plant with long woody stems, often hanging between trees in big loops

logging Chopping down the forest to sell the trees for timber

luminous Glowing in the dark

malaria Serious disease, carried by mosquitoes, causing high fever and even death

mangroves Trees that grow in the salty water of muddy swamps where rivers meet the sea

mimicry Pretending to be something else; a type of camouflage

nectar A honey-like drink produced by flowers to attract birds and insects

nocturnal Active at night

nutrient A kind of plant food

oxygen One of the gases found in the air, needed by all living things

parasite A plant or animal that feeds on another living plant or animal

pioneer Short-lived plant that grows when a gap appears in the forest

pitcher plant Insect-eating plant that grows on poor soil

pollen Sticky powder passed from one flower to another by birds and insects

predator An animal that hunts and kills others

prey An animal that is killed and eaten by a predator

rainforest Ancient forest found in parts of the world where the climate is always hot and wet

reptile Scaly, cold-blooded animal such as a lizard, snake or crocodile

sapling Young tree

saprophyte Something that feeds on dead or decaying matter

shrub Woody plant with many stems, usually not very tall

species A particular type of plant or animal

strangler A tree that wraps its roots around another tree for support

termite Tiny insect that eats dead wood and rotting leaves

understorey The layer of forest trees and shrubs between the ground and the canopy

vegetation The green parts of the forest

Index

Picture Acknowledgements

Juan Pablo Moreiras:
title page; 7tr; 11b; 18-19c; 21tr; 24-25c; 25r; 29tr; 32bc; 32-33c; 34c; 36-37 both; 38tr; 39l; 42bl; 42-43 background; 46l and tr

Tim Knight:
2-3c; 5br; 6b; 8-9 all; 10 both; 11tr; 12-13 all; 14-15 all; 16-17 all; 18l and c; 19tr and br; 20c and 20-21c; 22-23 all; 24bl and c; 26-27 all; 28 all; 29c and b; 30-31 all; 32l; 33c; 34-35c; 35t and b; 38b; 39br; 40-41all; 42cr; 43tr; 44-45 all; 47r

Richard Clemence:
4c; 5c

We would also like to gratefully acknowledge the following:

Jessica Creak and Aaron Chan pages 4-5
YHA Adventure Shops, Oxford, clothing and equipment, page 5
Wyld Court Rainforest, Newbury, Berkshire (photos: pages 13 t; 22b; 28tl; 30bl and cr; 35br)